GLORY SAYINGS

GLORY SAYINGS

Occasional Doxologies, Alternate Lyrics, and a Poem

REV. ROD RICHARDS

Hanje Richards

LEP

ISBN: 979-8-218-17360-9

Cover design: Lin Mercer   linmercer.net

Publication date: April 12, 2023, within the United States of America

First edition

Email all comments and inquiries to the author at minister.uuslo@gmail.com

I dedicate this book to the members and friends of Unitarian Universalists San Luis Obispo. The words in this volume are just a small piece of our ongoing conversation as we work together to deepen connections by nurturing spiritual growth, practicing justice, and inspiring joy.

Contents

How "Glory Sayings" Came to Be

Doxology – from the Greek: glory-saying. Usually refers to a hymn of praise, gratitude.

To the tune of Old Hundredth, the Doxology became a familiar piece of our services at UUSLO...possibly, a little too familiar. Even a hymn of praise can become routine after a while, and though we alternated among a handful of different lyrics in the hymnal, they seemed to be generally untethered from the rest of the service.

I began to wonder what it would be like if the lyrics were crafted to align with each service more closely such that—singing the well-remembered tune—people may find themselves surprised (amused, delighted, intrigued, even shocked) by the words that they were singing.

So it is that, borrowing from the Greek roots, I have titled these "Glory Sayings," not because all of these fit the description of hymns of praise (or would ever be described as "glorious"), but because there is something glorious about the very fact that we can communicate about weighty matters in a handful of words that—sung aloud, together, for the first time--can sometimes inspire reflection, amusement, a smile, a tear, a connection...

For the magic of words (and for a congregation that is willing to sing along beautifully with this quirky preoccupation), I am deeply grateful.

I am also deeply grateful to my very talented wife, Hanje, a partner in life whose photography reminds me of the magic that exists beyond words. I am routinely stunned by what she captures and am slowly learning to pull myself outside the frame of the everyday to really see the world around me. Magic, indeed.

A collection of doxologies
and
inspiring photographs

I

Pack nothing ...

Pack nothing for the way ahead.
Let spirits rise but not the bread.
Our freedom lies within our sight.
We'll get there if we travel light.

2

So grateful ...

So grateful for this life we share;
We feel love's power everywhere.
This little light that's yours and mine;
Our mission is to let it shine.

3

The truth ...

The truth, they say, will make us free;
It's there if we have eyes to see.
Most times we only get a peek;
So find, we say, and you shall seek.

4

They say ...

They say wherever we may roam
There's nothing quite like coming home.
It matters not where we have been.
Home is the place that takes us in.

5

Co-ve-nant …

Co-ve-nant guides how I treat you.
Mission describes what we will do.
Vision looks out toward where we'll be.
U-ni-ta-ri-an trinity.

6

With voice ...

With voice and hand and mind and heart;
Stronger together than apart.
I give from every piece of me
When I commit wholeheartedly.

7

From all …

From all who dwell here on this earth,
Our thanks for all that gave us birth.
In Darwin's quest for what is true,
He offers us a wider view.

8

From ocean ...

From ocean deep to skies above,
Our lives are defined by our love;
It's deep within that we must delve,
If we would learn to love ourselves.

9

So grateful for ...

So grateful for this life we share;
For all the beauty everywhere.
For songs we sing, and silence, too.
For love that grows me and you.

10

Come come …

Come, come, whoever you may be.
Come into this community.
Come, be our guest. Make this your home.
Then welcome those still yet to come.

11

The Golden ...

The Golden Rule applies, it's true.
What I expect, I give to you.
What must exist 'tween you and me
Is R-E-S-P-E-C-T.

12

We strive ...

We strive for happiness, it's true.
For pleasure; satisfaction, too.
When techniques fail which we employ
We find ourselves surprised by joy.

13

An end ...

An end is where we're starting from.
To leave means we must first have come.
To come means leaving where we've been.
We're starting out from being in.

14

We arm ...

We arm ourselves with honesty
So we may search responsibly
To find within that which is true
Inspiring all that we will do.

15

We meditate …

We meditate to understand.
We try to clap with just one hand.
But Zen eludes us even so.
Enlightenment's more than we know.

16

From we ...

From we who dwell below the skies
Where some do sink and others rise;
We strive for greater equity
So all can claim their dignity.

17

Though life …

Though life holds great diversity
We share a source, a destiny.
One Earth warmed by a single sun.
It's possible: we could be one!

18

Just as ...

Just as we live, we'll someday die
We may not know the reason why
But life holds joys unspoiled by death
May we be grateful for each breath.

19

Repent! ...

Repent! Wake up! Prepare the way!
We all yearn for a brighter day.
It came upon a midnight clear.
If we but love, we'll find it here.

20

In finding …

In finding out what's true for me,
I do believe in what I see.
But what I see depends in part
On what I believe from the start.

21

The dead …

The dead are in the rustling trees;
In ocean waves, in autumn breeze.
In memories our love lives on.
Those who have died, they are not gone.

2 2

The Earth ...

The Earth is Mother to us all.
Children, awaken to the call.
Plants, animals, humanity:
We're all part of one family.

23

Watch ...

Watch what they do, hear what they say.
We're building bridges every day.
Reflecting, then, on what we do.
And holding fast to what is true.

24

Folks listen ...

Folks listen up when money talks
It roars, it shouts; it sometimes squawks.
But we can teach it what to say
By how we live our lives each day.

25

Good things ...

Good things will come to those who wait;
But patience is not my best trait.
Good things should have arrived by now.
I have a lot to learn from Lao.

26

I sing ...

I sing, "My country, 'tis of thee..."
Yet must acknowledge history;
Not stand for inequality
But, in resistance, take a knee.

27

To these ...

To these young lives, we dedicate
Community, we co-create
A space in which the spirit's free
To explore all that each can be.

28

The stone ...

The stone, it's said, was rolled away.
The tomb was empty on that day.
The darkness had been pierced by light.
And courage overcame the fright.

29

Our acts ...

Our acts of generosity
Touch lives beyond what we can see.
The kindness ripples out and then
We find that it returns again.

30

We all wish ...

We all wish that we could be wise.
But how to find where wisdom lies?
Is it behind, beyond, above,
Or simply shines through all who love?

31

The beauty …

The beauty which I do behold
Is also in my eye, I'm told.
For beauty transcends what we see
and finds a home in you and me.

32

Life's full …

Life's full of wonder, so they say.
It's round about us every day.
I often miss it, I confess.
Awaken me to awe-some-ness!

33

Good news …

Good news, it says, the angels brought.
"A child is born," they said, "fear not."
It came upon a midnight clear.
If we but love, we'll find it here.

34

No single ...

No single creed unites us all;
No holy book, no prophet's call.
With love, we are identified,
Pledging to draw the circle wide.

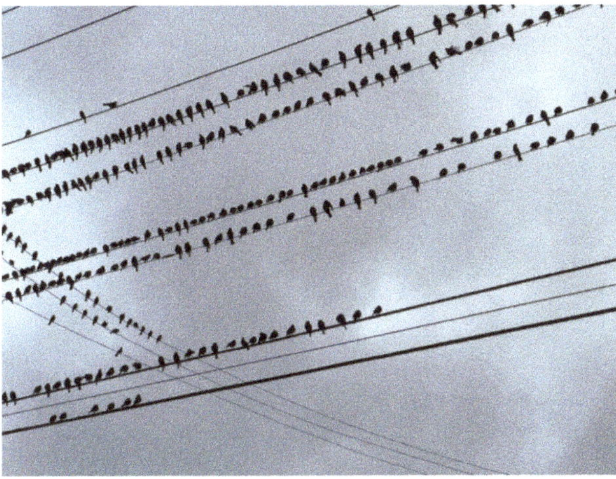

35

This virtual ...

This virtual reality
Has multiplied where we can be
Has altered when and what and how
And our attempts to "Be here now."

36

The old ...

The old year passes, let it go.
What this year brings, we've yet to know.
Yet, filled with possibility,
We celebrate it joyfully.

37

A way ...

A way is made where there's no way
One day's oil lasts beyond that day
Continues to sustain the flame
And love sustains us just the same.

38

Awake …

Awake and rise up from your bed,
New joy is waiting just ahead.
Though patience is not my best trait,
An-tic-i-pa-tion makes me wait.

39

All that ...

All that I do affects the whole
Denying that will take its toll
Wake, now, my senses to Earth's call
Connecting me to each and all.

40

Join 'round …

Join 'round the campfire, sing a song
Of love and hope, can that be wrong?
It's "Kumbaya" or "Come by Here"
Together, we erase the fear.

41

"We Won't Let Democracy Die"

I—like many of us, I am sure—often have songs running through my head. Sometimes, I actually remember the lyrics. Other times, I know I am just making my best guess (and hum through the places where I have no idea).

And then there are those times when remembered songs collide with reflections inspired by world events. In this case, the Channel Cluster Unitarian Universalist congregations were collaborating on a series of Zoom services focused on the theme of democracy. The 2020 election was just months away and the explicit attacks on voting rights were raising anxiety and fear, while also inspiring and mobilizing folks to "save our democracy."

I was holding the saddening realization that America has never really achieved the promise of a fully inclusive democracy along with the fear that the whole democratic experiment could be trashed in my time. I wanted to capture both that sadness and that promise...and so I wrote this.

"We Won't Let Democracy Die"

A long, long time ago
I can still remember how this country
Used to make me smile.
And I knew if I had my chance
I'd wrap my arms 'round its expanse
And that would make me happy for a while.

But reading hist'ry raised some questions
'Bout those childhood hist'ry lessons.
Discrimination at our founding
White supremacy abounding.

I have to say sometimes I cried
When I read about all those who tried,
Against the hate, to turn the tide.
I wonder: has democracy died?

But I---I won't let democracy die.
Let it be noted that I voted
    though the world's gone awry.

Self-evident truths can still expose the big lie
Sayin' I won't let democracy die.
We won't let democracy die.

For we choose to side with love
And if you have faith in God above
Seems to me She'd choose that, too.
And we do believe that justice rolls
As we rock the vote and work the polls
Staying far away from online trolls.

We could-when the outlook's this dim-
Throw in the towel and leave the gym.
Or we could keep up the fight
And shine a brand new light.

We're just some congregations doin' things
To build a world where hope still springs.
No matter what the future brings
We won't let democracy die.

That's why I promise I, I won't let democracy die
Let it be noted that I voted
      though the world's gone awry.
Self-evident truths can still expose the big lie

Singin' I won't let democracy die.
We won't let democracy die.

Sometimes we have to sing the blues
When we're so short on happy news
But listen: please don't turn away.
We need each voice here even more
As well as those who came before.
Our tears will do when we don't know
    what to say.

For on these streets, the homeless cope,
the migrants try, the children hope.
We trust those who've reflected
That we are all connected.

So we need to know our history
So we can transform society
Living toward that day we'll all be free
So democracy won't die.

But we'll keep singing, I, I won't let
    democracy die.
Let it be noted that I voted
    though the world's gone awry.

Self-evident truths can still expose the big lie.
I won't let democracy die.
We won't let democracy die.

We'll just keep singing
I, I won't let democracy die
Let it be noted that I voted
    though the world's gone awry
Self-evident truths can still expose the big lie
Singin, we won't let democracy die!

42

"We Shall Be Released"

As with "We Won't Let Democracy Die," this was a case where memories of songs that had been special to me collided with world events. Hearing the heart-wrenching details of what occurred in the shooting in Uvalde, Texas—echoing so many other needless, brutal shootings that have occurred in this country—caused me to wonder when we could ever expect an end to such events.

How many more "thoughts and prayers" platitudes from elected leaders who are committed to doing nothing to address these crimes can we bear? And, yet, my hope and my reading of history reminds me that people have the power. That change may take time, but it is possible, if we persist in our demands. Someday, things will change for the better. Any day now...

"We Shall Be Released"

(In memory of those who lost their lives at
Robb Elementary School in Uvalde, Texas on May
24, 2022...and too, too many others...)

They say a life can't be replaced,
They say each child is so dear.
And yet we can't shake the disgrace
Of what, again, has happened here.

Oh, may the light come shining
From the west down to the east.
Any day now, any day now
We shall be released.

They say every man needs protection,
That we need good guys with a gun.
But all I see is our inaction
And the tragedy of what's been done.

When will the light come shining
From the west down to the east?
Any day now, any day now
We shall be at peace.

Another leader urges us to pray
While we see pictures of the slain.
They warn us not to politicize
We suffer loss while they count gain.

Please let the light come shining
From the west down to the east.
Any day now, any day now
We shall be released.

This is no time for bowing heads,
No time to kneel and close our eyes.
It's time to make our voices heard
Above the clamor of the lies.

We'll be the light that comes shining
From the west down to the east.
This is the day now, today's the day now
We shall be released.

43

It is all very well ...

We, Unitarian Universalists, talk a lot about interdependence, connection, belonging, and inclusion. Don't get me wrong: these are all very important things. It's just that sometimes, I wonder how they are heard—how I am heard when I am talking about these things--by those people who may be suffering the deep pain of loneliness. (And who hasn't suffered loneliness at some time or another?) This poem was written in response to a call from Scott Tayler at Soul Matters for worship material on the monthly theme of Belonging.

It is all very well ...

It is all very well to speak of
an interdependent web of all life
and remind us that we are all
connected. We are.
But there are times when the loneliness
Strikes so deeply that the only
Thing of which I am
Certain is that I am
a
solitary
being.
There are times when the only
piece of belonging I can feel
is
the
longing.
There are times when the interdependent web
feels like just a mess of cobwebs
in a basement
or an attic
of the abandoned house

where I live...
Times when the spirit of life and love
are just words written
in invisible ink
on a postcard to myself.
Wish you were here.
Be with me now.
Don't try and talk me out
of how I feel
with perfect theology.
Stay beside me
and carry my hope
until I am ready to
hold it
again and be
there for
you.